REMOTE WORK, REAL PARENTHOOD

MAYA LOPEZ

REMOTE WORK, REAL PARENTHOOD

CONTENTS

EMBRACING REMOTE WORK AS A PARENT

The Rise of Remote Work

The rise of remote work has transformed the landscape for parents, especially those with young children. As more companies embrace flexible work arrangements, parents now have the opportunity to blend their professional responsibilities with the joys and challenges of raising a family. This shift allows parents to be present during critical moments of their children's early years, providing a unique chance to foster deeper connections while also pursuing their careers. The ability to work from home not only enhances the quality of family time but also opens the door to innovative strategies for balancing work and childcare.

One of the most significant advantages of remote work for parents is the ability to align work hours with their child's schedule. During nap times, parents can maximize productivity by tackling important tasks, attending virtual meetings, or catching up on emails. This focused work period can be a game-changer, allowing parents to accomplish essential work while still being mindful of their child's needs. By establishing a routine that takes advantage of these quiet moments, parents can create a harmonious balance that nurtures both their professional and parenting roles.

Creating a dedicated workspace in small homes can be a challenge, yet it is essential for maintaining productivity and focus. Designating a specific area as a workspace helps to establish boundaries between work and family life, allowing parents to mentally switch gears when needed. Simple solutions, like using a corner of a room or repurposing a closet, can transform any space into an efficient work area. By keeping this space organized and free of distractions, parents can make the most of their work hours while ensuring that their children feel secure and engaged elsewhere in the home.

Time management strategies are vital for parents navigating the demands of remote work and childcare. Utilizing tools like calendars and to-do lists can help parents prioritize tasks effectively. Setting realistic goals and breaking down projects into manageable steps can alleviate the pressure of juggling multiple responsibilities. Parents can also benefit from batching similar tasks together, allowing them to streamline their work processes and minimize interruptions. This proactive approach not only improves work efficiency but also allows parents to carve out precious moments for play and connection with their little ones.

Finally, the rise of remote work has prompted a greater need for supportive policies aimed at parents. Companies that recognize the challenges of working from home with young children can implement flexible schedules, provide mental health resources, and encourage open communication about work-life balance. As working parents navigate their dual roles, it is essential to foster an environment that supports their unique needs. By advocating for remote work policies that prioritize family well-being, parents can thrive both at work and at home, turning the challenges of remote work into opportunities for growth and fulfillment.

Benefits of Working from Home with Young Children

Working from home with young children presents a unique set of advantages that can greatly enhance the experience of parenthood while maintaining a career. For many parents, the flexibility of remote work allows them to be present for key moments in their child's early development. The ability to attend to a crying baby or participate in playtime without the constraints of a traditional office environment means that parents can nurture their children while continuing to fulfill their professional responsibilities. This dual engagement fosters a deeper bond and enriches family life, making it a rewarding experience for both parents and children.

One of the most significant benefits of remote work is the flexibility it offers in managing daily routines. Parents can align their work schedules with their children's nap times or playtimes, creating opportunities to focus on tasks without distractions. By strategically planning work around these moments, parents can maximize productivity while ensuring they are available for their little ones. This approach not only enhances time management skills but also encourages a healthier work-life balance, essential for maintaining overall well-being.

Creating a dedicated workspace at home, even in small living spaces, can enhance productivity and provide a sense of structure. By designating a specific area for work, parents can mentally separate their professional responsibilities from family life. This separation is crucial for maintaining focus and minimizing distractions, allowing parents to work efficiently while being physically close to their children. A well-thought-out workspace can also serve as a positive example for children, teaching them about the importance of organization and discipline from a young age.

Keeping babies entertained while working is another area where creativity can flourish. Parents can incorporate various activities that engage their children, such as sensory play or interactive toys, which allow them to explore independently. Utilizing age-appropriate activities not only keeps babies occupied, but it also supports their development. Parents can feel reassured knowing that their children are learning and growing while they attend to their work, merging the roles of caregiver and professional seamlessly.

Finally, prioritizing mental health is essential for parents navigating remote work with young children. Establishing a routine that includes breaks for self-care can make a significant difference in overall mood and productivity. Parents should not hesitate to reach out for support, whether through virtual parenting groups or professional counseling services. Embracing the challenges of remote work while raising young children can be daunting, but with the right strategies and support systems in place, parents can thrive both at home and in their careers, creating a harmonious and fulfilling family life.

Overcoming Initial Challenges

Overcoming initial challenges when transitioning to remote work with young children can feel daunting, but with some proactive strategies, it can also be an opportunity for growth and connection. Many parents experience a whirlwind of emotions as they juggle professional responsibilities and the demands of caring for a baby or toddler. Recognizing that it's perfectly normal to feel overwhelmed is the first step. Embrace this journey with the understanding that every challenge presents a chance to find creative solutions that work for your unique situation.

Creating a dedicated workspace in a small home can be one of the biggest hurdles for parents. The key is to carve out a specific area that signals to both you and your child that it's time for focused work. Even a small corner of a room can be transformed with a few thoughtful touches, such as a desk, a comfortable chair, and some personal decor. This not only helps to separate work from family life physically but also mentally prepares you to enter a productive mindset. Involving your child in this process can also be beneficial, as it allows them to understand that while you are present, certain times are dedicated to work.

Time management strategies become essential when navigating the complexities of remote work and childcare. One effective technique is to identify your peak productivity hours and align them with your child's nap schedule. Utilize these quiet moments to tackle your most challenging tasks. Additionally, consider creating a daily routine that incorporates blocks of focused work time interspersed with intentional playtime with your child. This not only boosts your productivity but also strengthens your bond with your little one, as you can fully engage during those designated moments.

Keeping babies entertained while you work is another initial challenge that many parents face. Stocking up on toys that promote independent play can be a game-changer. Look for items that capture attention and encourage exploration, such as sensory bins or stacking toys. Rotate these toys regularly to maintain your child's interest. Furthermore, exploring online resources for engaging activities can provide you with inspiration for fun and educational experiences that can keep your baby occupied while you attend to work tasks.

Lastly, remember the importance of mental health support for work-from-home parents. It's critical to acknowledge the emotional toll that balancing work and parenting can take. Establish check-in routines with yourself and seek out support networks, whether through online forums or local parenting groups. Sharing experiences and tips with fellow parents can provide a sense of solidarity and encouragement. By prioritizing your mental well-being, you empower yourself to tackle the challenges of remote work with resilience and creativity, ultimately creating a nurturing environment for both your professional growth and your child's development.

CHAP 2

CRAFTING YOUR
HOME OFFICE

Designing a Dedicated Workspace

Creating a dedicated workspace is essential for parents working from home, especially when balancing the demands of young children. Designing a space that separates your professional life from your home environment can significantly improve productivity and focus. Start by identifying a specific area in your home that can be transformed into your workspace, even if it's just a corner of a room. This area should be free from distractions and invite a sense of professionalism, allowing you to shift your mindset from parent to professional when you sit down to work.

When space is limited, it's important to be creative. Utilize vertical storage solutions, such as shelves or wall-mounted organizers, to keep your workspace tidy without taking up too much floor space. Consider using a small desk or a folding table that can be easily stored away when not in use. Personalize your workspace with motivational quotes or family pictures to make it feel inviting, but ensure that it remains functional. This balance will help you stay inspired while providing the structure necessary for focused work sessions.

Establishing boundaries within your dedicated workspace is crucial, particularly when young children are involved. Communicate to your family when you are in "work mode" by using clear signals, like a closed door or a designated sign. This helps your children understand that while you are physically present, you need to focus on work. Incorporate designated break times to check in with them and participate in quick activities, reinforcing your role as both a dedicated parent and professional.

Time management strategies can greatly enhance your ability to juggle work and childcare. Make use of your child's nap times or quiet playtimes to tackle important tasks that require deeper concentration. Create a flexible schedule that accommodates your family's rhythm, allowing you to maximize productivity while still being available for your child. Utilizing tools like timers can help you stay on track, ensuring that you make the most out of these precious moments of quiet.

Lastly, consider activities to keep your baby entertained while you work. Simple toys, sensory bins, or age-appropriate books can provide your child with engaging options while you focus on your tasks. Rotating toys regularly can keep their interest piqued and minimize distractions. Remember, it's okay to ask for help or explore remote work policies that support parents working from home. By implementing these strategies, you can create a harmonious environment where both work and family thrive, ultimately benefiting your mental health and overall well-being.

Small Space Solutions for Home Offices

Creating a functional home office in a small space can feel daunting, especially for parents of young children. However, with a little creativity and strategic planning, you can carve out a dedicated workspace that meets your professional needs without sacrificing your home's comfort. Start by assessing your home's layout and identifying underutilized areas, such as a corner in the living room, a nook in your bedroom, or even a spacious closet. By transforming these small spaces into work areas, you can establish a clear boundary between work and family life, helping you maintain focus during work hours while being present for your little ones.

Maximizing vertical space is a game changer when it comes to organizing a small home office. Consider installing shelves above your desk to store books, files, or decorative items that inspire you. Use wall-mounted organizers to keep essential supplies within reach, allowing for a clutter-free workspace. Remember to keep your desk minimalistic, with only the tools you need for work, so it doesn't become a catch-all for family items. This intentional design will help you stay organized and create an environment that fosters productivity, which is vital for balancing work and childcare.

Time management is crucial for parents working from home, particularly when juggling the unpredictable schedules of young children. Establishing a routine that aligns with your child's naps or quiet playtime can significantly enhance your productivity. Use these moments to tackle focused work tasks that require deep concentration. Additionally, consider using techniques like the Pomodoro method, where you work in short bursts followed by brief breaks. This approach not only helps maintain your focus but also allows you to sneak in quick moments with your child, ensuring you remain engaged in their world while fulfilling your professional responsibilities.

Keeping your baby entertained while you work is another essential aspect of managing a home office with young children. Create a designated play area nearby where your child can safely explore and play. Rotating toys and activities can keep them engaged longer, reducing interruptions during your work hours. Simple activities like sensory bins, stacking blocks, or even interactive storytime can provide meaningful engagement. By preparing these activities in advance, you can minimize distractions and create a more conducive work environment, allowing for quality productivity and quality parenting.

Finally, don't underestimate the importance of mental health support as you navigate the challenges of remote work and parenting. Connect with other parents, either online or in your community, to share experiences and strategies that work for you. Consider setting boundaries around your work hours to carve out time for self-care, whether that's a few quiet moments with a book, a quick exercise session, or even a virtual coffee with a friend. Remember, you are not alone in this journey, and fostering a supportive network can make a significant difference in your ability to balance work and parenting while maintaining your well-being.

Creating a Comfortable and Productive Environment

Creating a comfortable and productive environment is essential for parents navigating the challenges of remote work while caring for young children. An inviting workspace can make a significant difference in your daily routine, enabling you to focus on work tasks while being present for your little ones. Start by designating a specific area in your home as your workspace. Even in small homes, a corner of a room or a particular table can serve as your professional zone. Personalize this space with items that inspire you, such as photos, motivational quotes, or plants, to make it feel welcoming and energizing.

Establishing a routine can further enhance your work environment. Aligning your work hours with your child's nap times or playtimes can give you uninterrupted periods to focus on important tasks. Consider creating a visual schedule that outlines your work hours and your child's activities. This not only helps you stay organized but also communicates to your child when you are available for play and when you need focused time. Remember, flexibility is key; adjusting your schedule as needed will help you maintain productivity while ensuring your child feels secure and engaged.

To keep your baby entertained while you work, prepare a variety of activities that stimulate their senses and keep them occupied. Simple toys, sensory bins, or interactive play mats can be great distractions. Rotate these activities periodically to maintain your baby's interest, and don't hesitate to involve them in your work when appropriate. For instance, having them sit nearby with their toys while you attend a video call can help them feel included and less isolated, fostering a sense of togetherness even during busy work hours.

Time management strategies are crucial for parents balancing work and childcare. Utilize tools like timers or productivity apps to segment your work tasks into manageable chunks. The Pomodoro Technique, for example, encourages focused work sessions followed by short breaks, allowing you to check in with your child or attend to their needs. Incorporating small breaks to recharge and interact with your little one can boost both your mental health and productivity, creating a harmonious balance between work and parenting duties.

Lastly, prioritize your mental health as a fundamental aspect of your work-from-home environment. Establish boundaries between work and personal time to prevent burnout. Engage in self-care routines, whether it's a brief stretch, a quiet moment with a book, or a quick chat with a friend. Supportive remote work policies can also enhance your experience; advocate for flexibility in your work arrangements, and don't hesitate to seek out resources that promote mental well-being for parents. By creating a nurturing and productive environment, you can thrive both as a professional and a parent, finding joy in the journey of remote work and parenthood.

MASTERING TIME MANAGEMENT

Understanding Your Work Patterns

Understanding your work patterns is essential for parents navigating the challenges of remote work while caring for young children. Every parent has a unique rhythm, and recognizing your natural productivity peaks can help you align your work tasks with your childcare responsibilities. Take note of when you feel most focused and energized during the day, whether it's during your baby's morning nap or late at night after the household has settled. By understanding these patterns, you can structure your day in a way that maximizes your efficiency and allows you to be present for your little ones.

Creating a dedicated workspace, even in a small home, is crucial for establishing boundaries between work and family life. Identify a corner of your living space that you can transform into a functional office area. This could be a small desk in a quiet nook or a multi-use space that serves as both workspace and play area. Personalizing this space with motivational quotes or family photos can enhance your productivity and remind you of your purpose. When your children see you working in a defined area, they can learn to respect your work time while also understanding that you are available when needed.

Time management strategies play a pivotal role in balancing work and childcare. Implementing techniques like the Pomodoro Technique can help you work in focused bursts, allowing you to dedicate 25 minutes to a task followed by a short break. Use these breaks to engage with your child, take care of household tasks, or simply recharge. Additionally, it's helpful to plan your week ahead by prioritizing tasks and setting realistic goals. This proactive approach can alleviate the stress of feeling overwhelmed and increase your sense of accomplishment as you check items off your list.

Keeping babies entertained while you work can be a creative challenge, but there are numerous activities that can keep your little ones engaged. Consider setting up a sensory play area with safe toys, textured materials, or even simple household items that encourage exploration. Rotate toys regularly to maintain their interest, and consider short, interactive video calls with family members to provide a change of pace. These strategies not only aid your productivity but also support your child's development, fostering independence as they learn to play on their own.

Lastly, mental health support is vital for parents working from home. It's easy to feel isolated or overwhelmed, so prioritize self-care by scheduling time for yourself, even if it's just a few moments of mindfulness during your child's nap. Connect with other parents through online forums or local groups, sharing experiences and tips that can lighten your load. Remember, it's okay to ask for help or take a break when you need it. Embracing your work patterns while nurturing your mental well-being will create a more balanced environment for both you and your family, allowing you to thrive as a working parent.

Effective Scheduling Techniques

Effective scheduling techniques are essential for parents navigating the challenges of remote work while caring for young children. One of the first steps in establishing an effective schedule is to find a rhythm that works for both you and your baby. Understanding your child's natural routines can help you identify optimal work periods. Pay attention to their sleeping patterns, feeding times, and play schedules. By aligning your most focused work tasks with their nap times or quiet play sessions, you can maximize productivity while still being present for your child.

Creating a dedicated workspace, even in a small home, can significantly boost your ability to concentrate and manage your time effectively. Designate a specific area in your home as your workspace, if possible, away from distractions. This could be a corner of a room with a small desk or even a well-organized space on the dining table. Make it comfortable and inviting, and surround yourself with items that inspire productivity. When you have a clear boundary between work and home life, it becomes easier to switch into work mode when you need to focus, while also allowing you to be fully present with your child during breaks.

Time management strategies play a crucial role in balancing work and childcare. Utilizing tools like calendars, to-do lists, and timers can help structure your day. Break your work into manageable chunks and set specific goals for each session. Consider the Pomodoro technique—working in short bursts followed by short breaks—to maintain focus while allowing time for quick interactions with your little one. Remember, flexibility is key. There will be days when your schedule goes off track, and that's okay. Embrace the unpredictability that comes with parenting and adapt your plans as needed.

Keeping babies entertained while you work can be a challenge, but it's also an opportunity to engage their curiosity. Stockpile a variety of toys, books, and activities that can capture their attention for short periods. Rotate these items regularly to keep them fresh and exciting. Simple activities, like a sensory bin or a safe play area filled with colorful toys, can provide your child with independent playtime. You might also consider incorporating interactive video calls or virtual playdates with family members, allowing your child to enjoy social engagement while you grab some uninterrupted work time.

Finally, it's essential to prioritize mental health and self-care as you juggle the demands of remote work and parenting. Establishing a routine that includes short breaks for yourself can help recharge your energy. Use these moments to stretch, meditate, or simply enjoy a quiet cup of tea. Don't hesitate to reach out for support, whether from friends, family, or online communities of fellow work-from-home parents. Sharing experiences and tips can lighten the load and remind you that you are not alone in this journey. By adopting effective scheduling techniques, you can create a harmonious balance between work and family life, ensuring that both you and your child thrive.

Prioritizing Tasks and Responsibilities

In the journey of remote work while parenting young children, prioritizing tasks and responsibilities is crucial for creating a harmonious balance between work and family life. For parents navigating the demands of babies and professional obligations, it's essential to identify the most pressing tasks and allocate time effectively. Begin by listing all your responsibilities, both work-related and personal. This comprehensive view will help you see which tasks need immediate attention and which can be scheduled for later. Remember, it's not just about getting everything done; it's about focusing on what truly matters in the moment.

When working from home, the key to effective prioritization is understanding your and your child's rhythms. Take advantage of your baby's nap times or quiet play periods to tackle high-priority tasks. This strategy not only allows you to concentrate without interruptions but also reinforces the sense of accomplishment that comes from completing important work. By aligning your work schedule with your child's natural routines, you can create a more productive environment, making the most of those precious quiet moments.

Creating a dedicated workspace, even in a small home, can significantly enhance your ability to prioritize effectively. Designate a specific area for work that is separate from family spaces. This physical distinction helps you mentally shift gears between parenting and professional duties. Ensure this workspace is organized and equipped with essential tools, so when you sit down to work, you can dive right into your tasks without unnecessary distractions. A well-defined workspace signals to both you and your child when it's time to focus, fostering a sense of structure.

In addition to managing your time wisely, consider incorporating engaging activities for your baby that can keep them entertained while you work. Simple toys, sensory play, or even short videos designed for infants can provide you with those crucial minutes to complete work tasks. It's always a good idea to have a variety of options ready to sustain your child's interest, giving you the breathing room needed to focus on work without constant interruptions. Remember, it's perfectly okay to embrace a little screen time or structured play to create balance.

Lastly, don't underestimate the importance of mental health support in your remote work journey. Prioritizing self-care is vital for maintaining the energy and focus needed to juggle work and parenting. Establish a routine that includes breaks, even if they are brief, to recharge. Lean on support networks, whether through virtual meetups or online communities, where you can share experiences and strategies with other parents. By fostering a supportive environment, both personally and professionally, you empower yourself to prioritize effectively and thrive in this unique phase of life.

BALANCING WORK AND NAPTIME

Utilizing Nap Times Efficiently

Utilizing nap times efficiently can be a game changer for parents working from home. As any parent knows, the brief windows of peace during a baby's nap can feel like precious gems in a busy day. Embracing these moments not only aids in maintaining productivity but also allows parents to recharge and focus on their responsibilities. By planning tasks around these nap times, parents can create a more structured environment that benefits both their professional and personal lives.

First, consider prioritizing your to-do list based on urgency and complexity. Use the time when your baby is asleep to tackle the most demanding tasks that require deep concentration, such as writing reports, attending virtual meetings, or completing projects with tight deadlines. By aligning your workload with your child's nap schedule, you can maximize productivity and feel a sense of accomplishment when your little one wakes up. This strategy can help in reducing stress and managing your time effectively, allowing you to fully engage with your child during their awake hours.

Creating a dedicated workspace in a small home can also enhance your ability to utilize nap times efficiently. Designate a specific area for work that minimizes distractions and helps you transition into a productive mindset. Whether it's a corner of a room with a small desk or a cozy spot on the couch, having a defined workspace can signal to your brain that it's time to focus. When your baby falls asleep, you can quickly settle into this space, making the most of every minute without the hassle of setting up your workspace each time.

In addition to structured work tasks, consider incorporating activities that keep your baby entertained while you work during their awake times. Simple toys, sensory play, or even engaging them with music or storytime can provide you with short bursts of uninterrupted work. This proactive approach not only keeps your child happily occupied but also allows you to maintain a rhythm in your workday, ensuring that you are present both as a parent and a professional.

Lastly, remember to take care of your mental health throughout this balancing act. It's easy to feel overwhelmed when juggling work and parenting, especially in the confines of your home. Schedule moments for self-care during nap times, whether it's a quick meditation session, a cup of tea, or a few minutes of stretching. By prioritizing your well-being, you'll be better equipped to handle the demands of both work and parenthood. Embracing these strategies can lead to a more harmonious work-life balance, making the journey of remote work and parenthood a rewarding experience for you and your child.

Setting Realistic Work Goals

Setting realistic work goals is essential for parents navigating the challenges of remote work with young children. When you're balancing the demands of a job with the needs of a baby, it's important to establish achievable objectives that consider your unique circumstances. Start by identifying what is feasible within your available time, taking into account your child's nap schedule and the moments when they are most engaged. This approach not only minimizes stress but also allows you to celebrate small victories, making your work experience more fulfilling.

Creating a structured work environment, even in a small home, can significantly enhance your productivity. Designate a specific area as your workspace, even if it's just a corner of a room. This helps to mentally separate work from home life and signals to your family that you are in work mode. Within this space, set clear, daily work goals that can be easily tracked. For instance, break larger tasks into smaller, manageable segments that align with your child's routine, ensuring that you can maintain focus and progress without overwhelming yourself.

Time management is another crucial aspect of setting realistic work goals. Utilize your child's nap times effectively by planning your most demanding tasks during these quiet periods. Consider using timers to create focused work intervals, followed by short breaks to recharge. This technique not only keeps you on track but also allows you to be present with your baby when they wake up. By recognizing and utilizing these pockets of time, you can maintain a balance between your professional responsibilities and parenting duties.

Engagement strategies for your baby during work hours can also make achieving your goals more realistic. Having a repertoire of entertaining activities ready, such as sensory play, interactive toys, or even video calls with relatives, can keep your child happily occupied while you focus on work. This proactive approach not only ensures that your little one is entertained but also reduces the likelihood of interruptions, allowing you to meet your work objectives without feeling guilty about your parenting responsibilities.

Finally, remember that mental health is key to sustaining your ability to set and achieve work goals. Acknowledge that it's okay to adjust your expectations as needed. Seek support from fellow parents, online communities, or workplace resources to share experiences and strategies. Regularly reassess your goals and make adjustments that reflect your evolving situation. By creating a realistic framework for your work life, you can foster a positive environment that supports both your professional ambitions and your role as a devoted parent.

Transitioning Between Work and Parenting

Transitioning between work and parenting can often feel like a high-wire act, especially for parents of young children and babies. The delicate balance of meeting professional obligations while nurturing a little one requires flexibility and creativity. It's important to establish a routine that accommodates both work and caregiving, allowing you to embrace the joys of parenting without sacrificing your professional aspirations. By setting realistic expectations and understanding that both roles are interconnected, you can create a harmonious environment that supports your dual responsibilities.

Creating a dedicated workspace, even in a small home, is essential for maintaining focus and productivity. Designate a specific area where you can work, away from the distractions of family life. This doesn't mean you need a separate office; a corner of the living room or a cozy nook in your bedroom can work just as well. Equip your workspace with the necessary tools and resources that make your work efficient. Having a clear boundary between work and home life helps signal to both you and your child when it's time to focus on work, and when it's time to engage in play or relaxation.

Time management becomes a critical skill when juggling work and childcare. Nap times can be a golden opportunity to catch up on tasks, but it's also essential to prioritize your well-being. Consider creating a flexible schedule that allows for focused work sessions during these quieter moments, while also incorporating breaks to recharge. Use tools like timers or productivity apps to keep track of your time and tasks, ensuring you stay on top of your responsibilities without feeling overwhelmed. Embracing a flexible mentality will enable you to adapt as needed, whether your little one has an unexpected wake-up or requires more attention.

Keeping babies entertained while you work is another key aspect of this transition. Simple activities, such as sensory play or interactive toys, can capture your child's attention, allowing you to focus on your tasks. Look for engaging resources that encourage independent play, giving you the freedom to concentrate on work. Incorporating short, interactive breaks to play with your baby in between work sessions can strengthen your bond and provide the mental break you need. Remember, it's okay to ask for help from partners or family members when needed, allowing you to dedicate time to your work without neglecting your child's needs.

Lastly, mental health support is crucial for parents navigating the challenges of remote work and childcare. Make it a priority to carve out time for self-care, whether through short meditation sessions, exercise, or simply enjoying a cup of tea in silence. Connecting with other parents can also provide a sense of community and encouragement. Seek out groups or online forums where you can share experiences and tips with others in similar situations. Recognizing that you're not alone in this journey can offer immense comfort and support, reminding you that it's possible to thrive both as a parent and a professional in these unique circumstances.

KEEPING BABIES ENTERTAINED

Engaging Activities for Young Children

Engaging activities for young children can serve as a lifeline for parents working from home, allowing them to balance their professional responsibilities with the needs of their little ones. When you're juggling remote work and parenting, finding creative ways to keep your child entertained can make a significant difference. Simple yet engaging activities can capture a child's attention, providing busy parents with those precious moments of focus needed to tackle work tasks. These activities not only keep children occupied but also promote their development and creativity.

One effective approach is to create a structured playtime routine that aligns with your work schedule. Introducing a variety of activities, such as sensory bins, art projects, or interactive storytime, can keep your child engaged while you handle calls or complete tasks. Sensory bins filled with rice, beans, or water beads can captivate a toddler's curiosity and encourage independent play. Art projects, where children can explore colors and textures with minimal supervision, are great for fostering creativity and self-expression. Incorporating these activities into a daily routine allows children to anticipate playtime, making it easier for parents to plan their work around these engaging moments.

Utilizing nap times effectively is another strategy that can help parents manage their workload while ensuring their child has fun. During naps, consider setting up activities that require less supervision, such as puzzles or building blocks, for when your child wakes up. This approach allows you to complete critical tasks while your child enjoys quiet, independent play. Additionally, establishing a designated play area in your workspace can encourage children to engage in activities nearby while you work. This not only promotes a sense of security but also fosters the idea that both work and play can coexist harmoniously.

To further enhance your child's engagement, consider rotating activities regularly. Children thrive on novelty, and introducing new toys or crafts can spark their interest. Simple things like changing the layout of their play area or providing them with different materials can refresh their play experience. This rotation can be a fun way for parents to involve their children in the process, allowing them to help select what to explore next. Such involvement nurtures a sense of ownership and excitement, making playtime feel special and tailored to their interests.

Finally, remember that engaging activities can also be an opportunity for connection. Incorporating family playtimes into your schedule, even if brief, can reinforce your bond with your child. Activities that involve both parent and child, such as dance parties or quick games, create moments of joy that break up the workday and recharge your spirits. These shared experiences not only enrich your child's day but also enhance your own mental well-being. By integrating engaging activities into your daily routine, you create a nurturing environment that supports both your professional ambitions and your child's developmental needs.

Creating a Safe Play Area Nearby

Creating a safe play area nearby can significantly enhance your experience as a parent working from home. When you have a designated space for your young children to play, it not only keeps them engaged but also allows you to focus on your work with peace of mind. Start by choosing a corner of your home that is easily visible from your workspace. This proximity will let you keep an eye on your little ones while ensuring they are safe and entertained. Use soft mats or blankets to create a comfortable surface for play, and surround the area with age-appropriate toys that stimulate their curiosity and creativity.

Consider incorporating a variety of activities into this play area to cater to your child's interests and developmental stages. Rotating toys and materials regularly can keep the environment fresh and exciting for your child, encouraging independent play. Simple options like building blocks, soft books, or stacking cups can provide hours of entertainment. Additionally, organizing the space so that everything is within your child's reach promotes autonomy and helps them feel empowered, allowing you to focus on your tasks while they explore.

Safety should always be a priority when creating a play area. Ensure that the environment is free from hazardous items and sharp corners, and use safety gates if necessary to define boundaries. Secure any heavy furniture to the wall to prevent tipping, and keep small objects that pose choking hazards out of reach. By taking these precautions, you can create a safe space where your children can play freely, giving you the confidence to concentrate on your work without constant worry.

As your children grow and their needs change, be prepared to adapt the play area accordingly. Introducing new challenges, such as puzzles or art supplies, can help foster their development while keeping them engaged. Additionally, consider setting a routine where playtime coincides with your work tasks. For instance, you could plan for them to play independently during your most focused work blocks, such as during their nap times or quiet hours. This strategy not only helps you manage your time effectively but also teaches your children the value of independent play.

Creating a safe play area nearby is not just beneficial for your work-life balance; it also nurtures your child's development and well-being. By providing a dedicated space where they can explore and learn, you foster their creativity and independence. Remember to celebrate the small victories, both in your professional tasks and your parenting journey. Embracing this balance will not only enhance your productivity but also strengthen the bond with your child, making remote work a rewarding experience for both of you.

Using Technology Wisely

Using technology wisely is essential for parents working from home, especially when juggling the demands of a job with the needs of a young child. Embracing the right tools can streamline daily tasks and create a more efficient environment for both work and parenting. Start by identifying applications and platforms that enhance productivity while also allowing you to stay connected with your little one. For instance, using project management tools can help you organize your tasks, ensuring that you remain focused during your working hours while keeping your responsibilities clear.

Balancing work and childcare during nap times can be a game-changer for your productivity. Utilize technology to your advantage by setting reminders or timers that alert you when it's time to check on your baby. Consider using sound machines or baby monitors that connect to your smartphone, providing peace of mind as you work. This way, you can maximize your time during those precious moments of quiet, while also keeping a close watch on your child's needs.

Creating a dedicated workspace in small homes can be a challenge, but technology can help you design a functional area that promotes focus. Use online resources to find creative storage solutions and ergonomic designs that fit your space. Consider investing in noise-canceling headphones or a portable office setup that can be easily moved depending on where you find yourself working most efficiently. By establishing a workspace that meets your needs, you can foster a better work-life balance while feeling more productive.

Time management strategies are crucial for parents working from home. Leverage scheduling apps that allow you to block out time for work, childcare, and personal breaks. These tools can help you visualize your day and prioritize tasks effectively. Additionally, consider using shared calendars to coordinate with your partner or support system, ensuring that both of you can share responsibilities and keep track of important appointments or deadlines. This collaborative approach not only optimizes your time but also strengthens your support network.

Finally, keeping babies entertained while you work is a common challenge that can be addressed with thoughtful planning. Technology offers numerous resources, from engaging educational apps to interactive videos designed for young children. Select activities that encourage independent play but also allow you to maintain focus on your work. Additionally, consider incorporating screen time in moderation, using it as a tool to give yourself a break while also providing your child with stimulation. Remember, it's okay to seek mental health support when needed, so don't hesitate to reach out to fellow parents or professionals for guidance. By using technology wisely, you can create a nurturing environment that supports both your career and your family life.

DEVELOPING FAMILY-FRIENDLY REMOTE WORK POLICIES

Understanding Your Rights as a Working Parent

Understanding your rights as a working parent is crucial in navigating the challenges of remote work while raising young children. As you balance the demands of your job and the needs of your baby, it's essential to know the legal protections and workplace policies that can support you. Many countries have laws in place that aim to protect working parents, including the right to request flexible working arrangements, parental leave, and protections against discrimination. Familiarizing yourself with these rights can empower you to advocate for yourself and create a work environment that accommodates your parenting responsibilities.

As you work from home, it's vital to create an atmosphere that fosters productivity while also being mindful of your child's needs. Knowing your rights can help you negotiate a dedicated workspace, even in small homes, where you can concentrate on work while ensuring your child is safe and entertained nearby. Consider discussing with your employer the possibility of flexible hours that align with your child's nap times or play schedules. This proactive approach not only helps you manage your time better but also reinforces your commitment to maintaining a healthy work-life balance.

Time management becomes an essential skill for parents working from home, and understanding your rights can provide the confidence to implement effective strategies. For instance, you might have the right to request reasonable adjustments to your workload during particularly demanding parenting phases. By communicating openly with your employer about your responsibilities at home, you can work together to create a schedule that accommodates your role as a parent while allowing you to fulfill your professional duties effectively.

Keeping your baby entertained while you work is another area where understanding your rights can be beneficial. Many employers are increasingly aware of the challenges faced by working parents and may offer resources or programs to assist you. Whether it's access to childcare support or parent-focused initiatives, don't hesitate to explore these options. Engaging in activities that can hold your baby's attention while you focus on work is also a valuable strategy. Consider incorporating sensory play or interactive toys that will keep your little one busy, giving you the peace of mind to concentrate on your tasks.

Lastly, mental health support is an essential aspect of your rights as a working parent. Remote work can sometimes lead to feelings of isolation or overwhelm, especially when juggling the complexities of parenthood. Many organizations are beginning to recognize the importance of mental health and may offer resources such as counseling services or support groups for parents. By reaching out and taking advantage of these offerings, you not only take care of your well-being but also set an example for your child about the importance of seeking help and maintaining a healthy work-life balance. Embracing your rights as a working parent will empower you to create a nurturing environment for both your family and your career.

Advocating for Supportive Policies

Advocating for supportive policies is crucial for parents of young children, especially those navigating the challenges of remote work. As parents, we often find ourselves juggling multiple responsibilities, from meeting deadlines to tending to our little ones' needs. It's essential to recognize that we need policies that genuinely accommodate our unique circumstances. By advocating for flexible work hours, parental leave, and childcare benefits, we can create an environment that not only supports our professional growth but also nurtures our children's development.

One way to make a compelling case for these policies is to share personal experiences with coworkers and employers. When discussing the challenges of balancing work and childcare, especially during those precious nap times, it is vital to highlight the impact of supportive policies. Many parents have found success in managing their responsibilities when they have the flexibility to adjust their schedules. By sharing these stories, we can foster a culture of understanding and compassion within our workplaces, encouraging decision-makers to implement changes that make a meaningful difference.

Creating a dedicated workspace at home can also be a focal point in advocating for supportive policies. In smaller homes, it can feel overwhelming to find a suitable area to work while keeping children entertained. Employers can help by providing resources or suggestions for setting up a productive workspace, such as stipends for ergonomic furniture or noise-canceling headphones. When parents feel comfortable and equipped to work effectively at home, they are more likely to be productive, leading to better outcomes for both the employee and the organization.

Time management strategies tailored for parents working from home can further strengthen our advocacy efforts. By showcasing successful methods like batching tasks or utilizing timers for focused work sessions, we can demonstrate how these practices benefit not only individual productivity but also overall workplace efficiency. When organizations recognize the importance of these strategies, they are more likely to support policies that allow parents to implement them without the stress of rigid schedules.

Lastly, mental health support must be a cornerstone of any advocacy for remote work policies. Working parents often experience heightened stress and anxiety, especially when balancing professional responsibilities with parenting. Encouraging employers to provide access to mental health resources, such as counseling services or wellness programs, shows a commitment to the well-being of their employees. By prioritizing mental health, we can create a healthier work-life balance, enabling parents to thrive both at work and at home. Together, we can advocate for the supportive policies that will make a meaningful difference in our lives and the lives of our children.

Creating a Flexible Work Schedule

Creating a flexible work schedule is essential for parents navigating the challenges of remote work while caring for young children. As you embark on this journey, it's important to recognize that flexibility is not just a luxury; it is a necessity that can empower you to thrive both professionally and personally. By designing a work schedule that accommodates your family's needs, you can create a harmonious balance that allows you to be present for your children while also meeting your career aspirations.

Start by assessing your peak productivity hours and aligning them with your child's routine. For many parents, the quiet moments during naps or playtime can provide a golden opportunity to focus on high-priority tasks. Utilize these windows to tackle critical projects or attend virtual meetings. Involving your partner in this planning process can also enhance your scheduling flexibility, allowing you to share responsibilities and create overlapping work periods that maximize efficiency.

Creating a designated workspace, even in a small home, is another crucial element in establishing a flexible work schedule. This space doesn't have to be extravagant; a small corner of your living room or bedroom can work wonders. The key is to make it a distraction-free zone where you can concentrate fully on work. By setting clear boundaries within your home, both you and your children will understand when it's time to engage in work activities and when to play, fostering a healthy respect for each other's time.

Incorporating activities that keep your baby entertained while you work is vital for achieving a successful balance. Consider creating a rotation of safe toys, interactive games, or sensory activities that can engage your little one. This not only provides them with stimulating experiences but also allows you the time to focus on your tasks. As they explore and play, you can remain present in the moment while still keeping an eye on them, ensuring that both your work and parenting responsibilities are met.

Finally, remember that a flexible work schedule is not just about managing time; it's also about prioritizing your mental health. Make it a point to schedule breaks for yourself throughout the day. Use these moments to recharge, engage in mindfulness practices, or simply enjoy a cup of tea. By maintaining a healthy work-life balance, you not only support your own well-being but also set a positive example for your children. Embrace the unique challenges of remote work and parenting, and know that with a thoughtful approach, you can create a fulfilling and flexible work schedule that works for your family.

PARENTING HACKS FOR THE BUSY PROFESSIONAL

Multitasking with Intention

Multitasking with intention is a crucial skill for parents working from home, especially those with young children. Balancing professional responsibilities with the demands of childcare can feel overwhelming, but with a strategic approach, it can be both manageable and rewarding. The key is to cultivate an environment where work and parenting coexist harmoniously. This begins with recognizing the unique challenges that arise when your workspace is also your home, and choosing to engage in multitasking that not only serves your professional goals but also enhances your relationship with your child.

Creating a dedicated workspace, even in a small home, is essential for effective multitasking. Designate a specific area in your home as your work zone. This could be a corner of your living room or a spare bedroom. Ensure that this space is organized and equipped with everything you need to minimize distractions. By establishing boundaries between work and home life, you signal to both yourself and your child when it's time to focus and when it's okay to play. This clarity helps create a rhythm that your child can learn to respect, allowing you to concentrate on work during critical hours, like nap times or playtime.

Time management strategies are also vital for parents attempting to juggle work and childcare. Use tools like calendars or apps to block out specific times for work tasks, as well as periods for engaging with your child. During those precious nap times, prioritize your most demanding tasks, knowing that you can dedicate quality time to your baby afterward. Consider setting small, achievable goals for each work session, which can help you maintain momentum and feel accomplished. This structured approach not only enhances productivity but also ensures that you are present and engaged with your child when it matters most.

Keeping your little one entertained while you work is another aspect of intentional multitasking. Incorporate activities that promote independent play, allowing your child to explore safely while you focus on your tasks. Simple toys, sensory bins, or storytime can capture their attention for short bursts, giving you the breathing space needed to tackle your work. Rotate toys regularly to keep things fresh and exciting for your child. This not only supports their development but also fosters a sense of autonomy, giving you the freedom to concentrate on your work without constant interruptions.

Finally, it's essential to prioritize mental health and well-being as you navigate the complexities of remote work and parenting. Encourage yourself to take breaks when necessary and practice self-care to recharge. Whether it's stepping outside for a moment of fresh air or practicing mindfulness techniques, these small acts of self-kindness can significantly impact your productivity and happiness. Remember, multitasking with intention is not about doing everything perfectly; it's about finding balance and being present in both your work and your parenting journey. Embrace this phase with confidence, knowing that you are capable of creating a fulfilling life that honors both your professional aspirations and your role as a parent.

Streamlining Household Tasks

Streamlining household tasks is essential for parents of young children, especially when balancing work and childcare from home. The first step in this process is to establish a clear daily routine that accommodates both work responsibilities and parenting duties. By designating specific times for work, play, and household chores, parents can create a structure that minimizes chaos and promotes productivity. Incorporating nap times into this routine can be particularly effective. Using these quiet moments to tackle essential tasks allows parents to maximize their efficiency while ensuring they remain available for their little ones when they wake.

Creating a dedicated workspace, even in small homes, is another crucial aspect of streamlining household tasks. This space should be organized and free from distractions, allowing parents to focus on their work. Simple modifications, such as using a corner of the living room or a small desk in a bedroom, can transform any area into an effective workspace. Having all necessary supplies within reach minimizes interruptions, enabling parents to maintain their workflow and attend to their children's needs when required. A clearly defined workspace not only enhances productivity but also sets a professional tone that helps parents mentally separate work life from home life.

Time management strategies play a pivotal role in balancing work and childcare. Parents can utilize techniques like time blocking, which involves scheduling specific periods for focused work, breaks, and childcare activities. This approach allows for a more organized day, where parents can anticipate challenges and allocate time accordingly. Additionally, leveraging tools such as digital calendars or task management apps can help keep track of deadlines and daily responsibilities. By establishing boundaries and prioritizing tasks, parents can navigate their workload more effectively, reducing stress and creating more quality time with their children.

Keeping babies entertained while working is another key element in streamlining household tasks. Parents can prepare age-appropriate activities that captivate their child's attention, allowing them to focus on work. Simple toys, sensory bins, or interactive games can provide entertainment while promoting developmental skills. Rotating toys and introducing new activities can sustain a child's interest and extend independent playtime. Moreover, incorporating short breaks to engage with the baby can create a harmonious balance, ensuring that both work and parenting needs are met without feeling overwhelmed.

Lastly, it's essential to acknowledge the importance of mental health support for work-from-home parents. Balancing work and childcare can be emotionally taxing, and seeking support through community resources, online groups, or professional counseling can provide valuable relief. Sharing experiences with other parents can also foster a sense of camaraderie, reducing feelings of isolation. Prioritizing self-care, whether through short breaks or engaging in hobbies, can recharge parents' energy and enhance their overall well-being. By streamlining household tasks and implementing supportive strategies, parents can create a nurturing environment that fosters both productivity and a loving atmosphere for their children.

Finding Time for Yourself

Finding time for yourself while juggling the demands of work and parenting can feel like an impossible task, especially for those working from home with a baby in the house. However, carving out even small moments for self-care is essential for your mental well-being and productivity. Start by recognizing that you are not alone in this challenge. Many parents share the struggle of finding balance, and it's important to prioritize your own needs alongside those of your children. Establishing a mindset that values self-care is the first step in reclaiming your time.

One effective strategy is to utilize your child's nap time to focus on your own needs. When your baby is asleep, it's tempting to dive straight into work tasks, but consider setting aside a few minutes for yourself instead. Use this time to engage in activities that rejuvenate you, whether it's reading, meditating, or simply enjoying a cup of coffee in peace. By intentionally reserving these short breaks, you will return to your work with renewed energy and focus, making you more efficient when your little one is awake.

Creating a dedicated workspace in your home, even if it's a small corner of a room, can significantly impact your ability to manage both work and childcare effectively. This space should be free from distractions and equipped with everything you need to work productively. When you establish boundaries between your work and personal life, you can better compartmentalize your time. This separation not only enhances your focus during work hours but also allows you to be fully present with your child during breaks.

Time management strategies play a crucial role in helping parents navigate their dual responsibilities. Implementing a daily schedule can provide structure to your day. Incorporate blocks of time for work, childcare, and self-care, and don't hesitate to be flexible when things don't go as planned. Prioritizing tasks and setting realistic goals will also help you stay on track. Remember, it's okay to ask for help from your partner or family members when needed. Delegating responsibilities can free up time for you to recharge.

Finally, consider engaging your baby in activities that can keep them entertained while you work. Simple toys, sensory play, or even a safe playpen nearby can provide you with short windows of time to focus on your tasks. This not only allows you to work effectively but also encourages your child's development. By integrating these strategies into your routine, you can create a harmonious balance that nurtures both your career and your well-being. Remember, taking care of yourself is not a luxury but a necessity for both you and your family.

SUPPORTING MENTAL HEALTH

Recognizing Signs of Stress and Burnout

Recognizing the signs of stress and burnout is crucial for parents navigating the challenges of remote work while caring for young children. The unique demands of balancing work and family life can sometimes lead to feelings of being overwhelmed. It's important to pay attention to both your emotional and physical well-being. Common indicators of stress may include irritability, fatigue, difficulty concentrating, and a sense of being constantly on edge. When these feelings start to creep in, it's a signal that your mind and body may need a break.

One of the first signs that you might be experiencing burnout is a loss of motivation. When you find it hard to engage in work tasks that once excited you or feel detached from your responsibilities, it's a sign that you need to reassess your workload and self-care routines. This can also manifest in your interactions with your children; if you notice that you are less patient or responsive to their needs, it's time to take a step back and evaluate how you can better manage your time and energy.

Physical symptoms can also reveal the toll that stress is taking on you. Headaches, muscle tension, and trouble sleeping are all signs that your body is signaling for help. Make it a priority to establish a dedicated workspace in your home, even if space is limited. This can create a boundary between your work and personal life, helping to alleviate some of the stress that comes from trying to juggle multiple roles in the same environment. Additionally, simple practices such as stretching or taking short walks during breaks can help mitigate these physical symptoms.

Mental health support is equally essential. Engaging with other parents through online communities or support groups can provide a safe space to share experiences and coping strategies. This connection can alleviate feelings of isolation, reminding you that you are not alone in this journey. Consider incorporating quick mindfulness exercises or breathing techniques into your routine, which can be particularly beneficial during those demanding moments when the baby is napping, and you have a few precious minutes to yourself.

Finally, embrace the idea of flexibility in your work routine. Understanding that some days will be more challenging than others can help you adjust your expectations. Create a list of activities to keep your baby entertained while you focus on work, allowing you to maintain productivity without sacrificing quality time with your child. Remember, it's perfectly okay to ask for help or delegate tasks when you need it. Recognizing these signs of stress and taking proactive steps will empower you to create a healthier, more balanced approach to remote work and parenting.

Strategies for Maintaining Mental Well-being

Creating a nurturing environment for both your mental well-being and your child's growth is essential, especially when navigating the unique challenges of remote work as a parent. One effective strategy is to establish a dedicated workspace in your home. This doesn't mean you need a large office; even a small corner can serve as a clear boundary between work and family life. Having a specific area where you focus on work helps signal to both your mind and your little one that it's time for concentration. Decorate this space with items that inspire you, making it a pleasant place to accomplish tasks while also being a reminder of your commitment to balancing work and parenting.

Time management is crucial when you're juggling work responsibilities with childcare. Consider implementing a structured schedule that aligns your work tasks with your baby's nap times. By planning your most demanding work during these quieter periods, you can maximize productivity while ensuring that your child receives the attention they need when they are awake. Using tools like timers or apps can help you compartmentalize your work hours, making it easier to switch from professional mode to parenting mode. Remember, it's okay to be flexible; if a nap doesn't go as planned, adapt your schedule as needed.

Keeping babies entertained while you work is another vital aspect of maintaining mental well-being. Engaging toys, simple games, or even interactive apps designed for young children can provide both stimulation and enjoyment for your little one. Rotate toys frequently to keep their interest piqued, and consider setting up a safe play area within your line of sight. Incorporate short, playful breaks into your workday where you can interact with your baby, helping to strengthen your bond and recharge your mental energy.

Multitasking is an inevitable part of being a parent who works from home, but it can be done effectively with a few practical hacks. For instance, you can involve your baby in simple activities while you work, such as having them sit next to you with a few toys or books. This not only keeps them entertained but also fosters a sense of companionship. Additionally, use your breaks wisely; a quick walk around the house or a fun dance session with your baby can work wonders for your mood and mental clarity.

Lastly, remember that prioritizing your mental health is not just beneficial for you but also for your child. Don't hesitate to reach out for support, whether through online communities, friends, or mental health resources specifically aimed at parents. Many workplaces now have policies in place that recognize the unique challenges of remote work for parents, so take advantage of those resources when needed. Balancing work and parenting is a journey, and by implementing these strategies, you are not only fostering your own well-being but also creating a loving and supportive environment for your child to thrive.

Building a Support Network

Building a support network is crucial for parents of young children navigating the challenges of remote work. As you balance the demands of your job with the needs of your little ones, having a robust support system can make a significant difference. This network can consist of family, friends, colleagues, and even online communities that understand the unique struggles of working parents. By reaching out and connecting with others, you can share experiences, exchange tips, and find reassurance that you are not alone in this journey.

One of the most valuable aspects of a support network is the exchange of practical advice tailored to your specific situation. For instance, parents can share strategies for managing work during nap times or suggest engaging activities to keep babies entertained while you focus on your tasks. These insights can help you optimize your day and create a more harmonious balance between work and childcare. Additionally, connecting with other parents can inspire you to develop your own parenting hacks, helping you multitask effectively while ensuring your child's needs are met.

Creating a dedicated workspace in a small home can be a challenge, but your support network can help. Friends and fellow parents can provide ideas on how to carve out a productive area within your living space that minimizes distractions, even when little ones are nearby. Sharing photos or layouts of their setups can spark creativity and encourage you to make the most of your environment. Remember, a well-defined workspace can foster focus and productivity, allowing you to thrive both as a professional and as a parent.

Time management strategies are another critical topic within your support network. Engaging with other parents who work from home can lead to the discovery of effective scheduling techniques that have worked for them. This could include setting strict work hours, using timers for focused tasks, or creating a shared calendar with your partner to coordinate responsibilities. By learning from one another's experiences, you can develop a routine that respects both your professional commitments and your family's needs.

Finally, mental health support is an essential component of any support network. Working from home with young children can be isolating and stressful, so it's important to have outlets for sharing your feelings and challenges. Look for online support groups or local meet-ups where you can connect with other parents who understand what you're going through. Sharing struggles and celebrating victories together can foster a sense of community and belonging, reminding you that you are part of a larger group navigating similar experiences. By building and nurturing your support network, you can create a more enjoyable, balanced, and productive remote work experience.

BUILDING A COMMUNITY OF SUPPORT

Connecting with Other Remote Parents

Connecting with other remote parents can be a lifeline for those navigating the challenging yet rewarding journey of working from home while caring for young children. In a world that often feels isolated, finding a supportive community can provide not only practical tips but also emotional encouragement. Engaging with fellow parents who share similar experiences can help alleviate feelings of loneliness and offer a space for sharing both struggles and successes.

One effective way to connect with other remote parents is through online forums and social media groups dedicated to working parents. These platforms allow for the exchange of ideas, resources, and personal anecdotes. By participating in discussions, you can learn from others' experiences regarding balancing work and childcare. Whether it's sharing strategies for keeping babies entertained during work hours or discussing effective time management techniques, these connections can help you feel more understood and supported in your daily challenges.

Additionally, consider organizing virtual meet-ups with other parents in your network or joining local parenting groups that have adapted to the digital age. These gatherings can provide a casual environment to share insights on creating dedicated workspaces in small homes or developing routines that maximize productivity during nap times. Collaborating with fellow parents can inspire new ideas and solutions that you may not have considered, ultimately enhancing your work-life balance.

For those who feel overwhelmed, connecting with other parents also opens avenues for mental health support. Sharing your experiences with others who are in similar situations can be incredibly validating. It creates a sense of community where you can discuss not only the joys of parenthood but also the stresses that come with juggling multiple responsibilities. This mutual understanding can foster resilience and provide motivation, reminding you that you are not alone in your journey.

Finally, don't underestimate the value of informal connections that can arise from your existing social circles. Reach out to friends or acquaintances who are also balancing remote work with parenting. These relationships can yield invaluable parenting hacks for multi-tasking while working and foster a sense of camaraderie. By building a network of fellow remote parents, you create a support system that enriches your experience, making the challenges of remote work and parenthood more manageable and enjoyable.

Sharing Resources and Tips

When navigating the complexities of remote work while caring for young children, sharing resources and tips can be invaluable. One of the most effective strategies is to create a dedicated workspace, even in small homes. Designate a specific area in your living space that signals to both you and your child that it's time for work. This could be a corner of the living room or a nook in the bedroom. By establishing this physical boundary, you not only enhance your productivity but also help your child understand the importance of your work time. Consider using furniture that can be easily rearranged as your needs change, allowing you to adapt your workspace without significant hassle.

Time management becomes crucial when balancing work and childcare. One effective approach is to align your work tasks with your child's nap schedule. Use these quiet moments to tackle the most demanding projects or attend important meetings. In addition, consider creating a flexible schedule that includes short bursts of focused work interspersed with quality time spent with your child. This balance can help maintain your productivity while also ensuring that your little one feels secure and cherished. Sharing your schedule with your partner or family members can also foster a supportive environment, allowing you to tag-team childcare duties effectively.

Keeping babies entertained while you work is another challenge that many parents face. It can be helpful to curate a list of engaging activities that your child can explore independently. Simple toys, sensory bins, or interactive apps can captivate their attention for a while, giving you precious moments to focus. Rotate these activities regularly to keep things fresh and exciting for your little one. Furthermore, consider setting up a play area that is safe and accessible, allowing your child to play nearby while you work. This way, you can keep an eye on them while still being productive.

Mental health support is essential for parents working from home. Establishing a network of fellow parents can provide a vital lifeline. Share experiences, resources, and tips to help each other navigate the ups and downs of remote work and parenting. Online communities, local groups, or even informal meet-ups can foster connections that alleviate feelings of isolation. Additionally, don't hesitate to reach out for professional mental health support if needed. Prioritizing your well-being not only benefits you but also sets a positive example for your child about the importance of self-care.

Lastly, implementing parenting hacks can significantly improve your ability to multitask. For instance, try incorporating educational videos or audiobooks into your child's routine during your work hours. This allows you to engage their minds while freeing up some of your time. Another helpful tip is to involve your child in simple tasks; for example, giving them a safe space to "work" alongside you with their own toys or art supplies can create a sense of teamwork. These small adjustments can lead to a more harmonious balance between your professional responsibilities and parenting duties, making the remote work experience more enjoyable and fulfilling for everyone involved.

Creating a Supportive Work Environment

Creating a supportive work environment is essential for parents juggling the demands of remote work and childcare. As you navigate the challenges of working from home with a baby, it's important to design a space that fosters productivity while accommodating the needs of your little one. A dedicated workspace, even in a small home, can help establish boundaries between professional responsibilities and family life. Consider utilizing corners or alcoves in your home to create a cozy office nook. This can be as simple as a small desk set up in a quiet area, surrounded by items that inspire you and promote focus.

When it comes to balancing work and childcare, time management becomes a crucial skill. Recognizing your baby's nap schedule can help you carve out uninterrupted work periods. Use these quiet moments to tackle your most demanding tasks. By planning your day around these natural breaks, you can maximize productivity while still being present for your child. Additionally, employing tools such as timers or task lists can keep you organized and ensure that you make the most of your available time.

Keeping your baby entertained while you work can also be a game changer. Explore a variety of engaging activities that promote independent play and allow you to focus. Simple toys, sensory bins, or even interactive play mats can capture your baby's attention while you tackle your work. Rotating these activities can keep them fresh and exciting, giving you the breathing room you need to concentrate. Also, don't hesitate to involve your baby in your work routine; they can be your little assistant, providing both joy and a sense of connection as you navigate your tasks together.

Developing remote work policies that support parents with young children is vital for fostering a collaborative and understanding workplace culture. Advocate for flexibility in your work schedule, allowing for adjustments when unexpected parenting demands arise. Suggest regular check-ins with your manager or team to discuss workload and share strategies that can help everyone balance their responsibilities. Creating an open dialogue about the unique challenges of parenting while working can lead to solutions that support not just you, but your colleagues as well.

Lastly, prioritizing mental health is essential for work-from-home parents. Create a routine that includes breaks for self-care, whether it's a short walk, a few moments of deep breathing, or simply stepping away from your workspace to recharge. Connecting with other parents in similar situations can provide invaluable support, sharing experiences and coping strategies. Remember, you're not alone in this journey; building a supportive community around you can make all the difference, allowing you to thrive both as a parent and a professional.

CELEBRATING SUCCESSES AND LEARNING FROM CHALLENGES

Reflecting on Your Journey

Reflecting on your journey as a working parent in a remote environment can offer profound insights into the challenges and triumphs you've experienced. Each day presents a unique set of hurdles, from managing work deadlines to soothing a fussy baby. It's essential to take a moment to acknowledge the resilience you've shown. By recognizing the small victories, such as completing a work task while your little one naps or successfully entertaining your baby with a simple activity, you can cultivate a sense of accomplishment that fuels your motivation.

As you navigate the complexities of balancing work and childcare, consider the strategies that have worked for you. Have you found that creating a dedicated workspace, even in a small home, helps you concentrate better? Perhaps you've developed a routine that allows you to maximize productivity during those precious nap times. Reflecting on these effective practices not only reinforces your ability to juggle responsibilities but also highlights the importance of adaptability in your role as a parent and a professional.

Moreover, think about the innovative parenting hacks you've discovered along the way. Whether it's using engaging toys or sensory activities to keep your baby entertained while you work, these little tricks can significantly ease the tension of multitasking. By sharing these insights with fellow parents, you contribute to a supportive community where everyone can learn from each other's experiences, fostering a sense of camaraderie that is so vital during these challenging times.

It's also crucial to recognize the importance of mental health support in your journey. Working from home with a baby can sometimes lead to feelings of isolation or overwhelm. Reflect on the times when you've sought help, whether through online parenting groups or by simply reaching out to a friend. These connections can provide not only emotional support but also practical advice on navigating remote work policies that cater to parents with young children. Remember, reaching out is a sign of strength, and it can make a world of difference in your daily routine.

Ultimately, reflecting on your journey allows you to appreciate how far you've come, both as a parent and as a professional. Embrace the lessons learned and the growth experienced through each challenge. By recognizing your achievements and the valuable skills you've acquired, you can foster a positive outlook that will benefit both your family and your career. Remember, you are not alone on this journey, and every step you take is a testament to your dedication and love for your child.

Adjusting Expectations and Embracing Flexibility

Adjusting expectations is a crucial first step for parents navigating the challenges of remote work with young children. It's important to accept that the ideal workday may look different when your toddler is home or your baby is napping. Recognizing that interruptions are part of the experience can ease the pressure parents often feel to maintain a traditional work environment. Instead of striving for perfection, focus on prioritizing key tasks and being flexible with your schedule. By setting realistic goals and allowing room for adjustments, you create a more sustainable work-life balance that honors both your professional responsibilities and your roles as a parent.

Embracing flexibility means finding creative ways to integrate work and childcare. Utilize your baby's nap times strategically; these precious moments can be ideal for tackling important projects or engaging in video calls. However, also be prepared for those unexpected moments when nap times don't go as planned. Having a backup plan, such as a quick activity or toy swap, can help keep your little one entertained, allowing you to maintain your focus. Furthermore, don't hesitate to tap into your support network—whether it be a partner, family member, or friend—who can lend a hand during peak work hours.

Creating a dedicated workspace in a small home can also play a vital role in managing expectations and fostering productivity. Designate a specific area in your living space that is free from distractions, even if it's just a small corner of a room. This separation helps signal to both you and your child that it's time for focused work, and it also creates a physical boundary that can minimize interruptions. Personalizing this workspace with items that inspire you or bring you joy can enhance your motivation, making it easier to transition into work mode amidst the chaos of parenting.

Time management strategies are essential for parents juggling work and childcare. Consider utilizing tools like time blocking to allocate specific hours for work tasks, breaks, and parenting duties. This structure can help you visualize your day and ensure you're dedicating time to both your professional obligations and quality moments with your child. Additionally, don't forget the value of self-care.

Carving out small breaks for yourself can recharge your energy and improve your overall well-being, making you more effective in both your work and parenting roles.

Finally, mental health support is vital for work-from-home parents. Recognizing that it's normal to feel overwhelmed at times can be reassuring. Seeking out resources—be it online communities, professional counseling, or wellness apps—can provide valuable support and connection. Sharing experiences with other parents can also foster a sense of solidarity and understanding. By prioritizing your mental health and embracing flexibility in your routines, you can navigate the complexities of remote work and parenting with grace, turning challenges into opportunities for growth and connection.

Inspiring Stories from Other Working Parents

In the journey of balancing work and parenthood, many working parents have found creative ways to thrive in their unique situations. One inspiring story comes from Sarah, a freelance graphic designer who transformed her small living room into a vibrant workspace. With a few simple adjustments, such as a dedicated desk area and organized storage, she created an environment that not only boosts her productivity but also keeps her focused during her baby's nap times. Sarah's ability to carve out this space illustrates how even in the tightest of quarters, parents can prioritize their work while remaining present for their children.

Another remarkable example is Tom, a full-time remote software engineer who has mastered the art of time management. He schedules his most demanding tasks during his baby's longest sleep stretches, taking advantage of quiet moments to focus deeply. By utilizing tools like timers and task lists, Tom has developed a routine that allows him to achieve his professional goals while ensuring he is available for playtime when his little one is awake. His approach shows that with careful planning, balancing the demands of work and childcare can lead to fulfillment in both areas.

Lisa, a marketing manager, has discovered innovative activities to keep her baby entertained while she works. By incorporating sensory play and educational toys into her workday, she engages her child in ways that stimulate development while allowing her to remain productive. Lisa's use of structured playtime not only enriches her child's experience but also fosters a sense of accomplishment in her own work. This dynamic exemplifies how parents can intertwine their responsibilities, creating a harmonious balance that supports both their children's growth and their career aspirations.

For many parents, the mental health aspect of remote work is critical. David, a project manager, prioritizes self-care by incorporating regular breaks into his schedule. He shares how stepping outside for fresh air, even if just for a few minutes, rejuvenates his mind and spirit. David emphasizes the importance of recognizing when to pause and recharge, reminding other parents that taking care of themselves is just as essential as caring for their children. His story serves as a reminder that maintaining mental well-being is crucial for sustaining productivity and positivity in a demanding environment.

Finally, the journey of working parents often includes learning from one another. Community support has been invaluable for many, as illustrated by Maria, who created a virtual support group for parents in her neighborhood. By sharing tips on remote work policies and parenting hacks, she has built a network that empowers members to exchange ideas and strategies. Maria's experience highlights the strength found in community, encouraging parents to reach out and connect with others who understand their challenges. Together, these stories demonstrate that while the path of working parents can be challenging, it is also filled with inspiration, creativity, and the potential for success in both professional and personal realms.